Early Intermediate

Audition Repertoire for the Intermediate Pianist

Two Stylistically Balanced & Technically Diverse Programs | Edited by Jane Magrath

MW00851446

Alfred Music Publishing Co., Inc.
P.O. Box 10003
Van Nuys, CA 91410-0003
alfred.com

ISBN-10: 0-7390-7950-6
ISBN-13: 978-0-7390-7950-8

The selections in this book are intended to provide music for the intermediate pianist that is motivating and balanced in terms of period contrast and style. The pieces are "tried and true" selections—piano works that have formed the basis of audition repertoire throughout the 20th and into the 21st centuries. For many years, performers at this level have enjoyed playing these pieces, which have become standards in the intermediate piano repertoire. I am sure that you'll find some of your favorites included here.

Audition Repertoire for the Intermediate Pianist, Book 1 contains two programs from which to choose to create a well-balanced audition, festival or recital program. Note the variety of composers, moods and musical characters within the pieces in each program. Most individuals will study one of the programs within a semester of piano study. Some individuals may work longer on the pieces, but it is best to choose a program that can be mastered within approximately one academic semester. Some may want to mix compositions between the two programs (however, note that the programs as presented are designed to be balanced).

To best learn these compositions, avoid practicing at a very slow tempo for too long. While slow practice of individual passages is desirable and necessary, a composition that is played under-tempo daily for too long (more than four to six weeks) may grow stale. In this case, the performer could lose his or her innate instinct for the underlying character of the work. It is also suggested that the performer memorize the pieces as early as possible. Please take time to study the editorial commentary on the scores (see page 3).

I hope that you derive as much pleasure from practicing and playing this music as I have. You are delving into the great art-literature for our instrument—what a great privilege and challenge!

Warm thanks and sincere appreciation to Morty and Iris Manus, Tom Gerou, Carol Matz and E.L. Lancaster for their support and help with this series.

A Special Note to the Performer

These pieces have been selected with the performer and his or her enrichment in mind. Best wishes for many days of delight, joy and beauty as you practice and perform these selections. Most importantly, learn to critique yourself by listening carefully as you play (be your own teacher while practicing), and enjoy every piece that you read or study!

Jane Magrath

EDITORIAL COMMENTARY

Trumpet Tune in C Major, ZT 698 (Purcell)

Purcell was an English composer during the Baroque era. He began composing at the age of nine and wrote a substantial number of works for harpsichord, including eight suites. He also left about 30 additional works for keyboard, including this piece. A work such as this was originally performed on a virginal or spinet, both of which are somewhat smaller than many harpsichords. In *Trumpet Tune*, one can hear the trumpets calling people to attention through the grand fanfare. Fingering, articulation and dynamics are editorial.

Sonatina in G Major, Anh. 5, No. 1 (Beethoven)

Beethoven was born in Bonn, Germany, but moved to Vienna in 1792 and spent the remainder of his life there. This work is among his shortest, and is one of five sonatinas he composed for piano. The short slurs in the first movement should be played distinctly. The form of each movement is: **A B A** codetta.

The Avalanche, Op. 45, No. 2 (Heller)

Heller was a close friend of Chopin, Schumann and Liszt, all of whom offered respect and encouragement. He wrote several hundred piano pieces, mostly in small forms. The *Études*, Op. 45–47 are among his most vital and important teaching pieces. Many of the études have been assigned titles (such as this one), which suggest mood or character. *The Avalanche*, perhaps the most popular selection from Heller's Opus 45, is an energetic piece that sparkles. Attention should be paid to producing even eighth notes in the ascending passages, and to playing resonant chords. The phrasing can become monotonous unless it is carefully worked out to show variety.

Petite Piece, Op. 6, No. 5 (Goedicke)

Goedicke served as a professor at the Moscow Conservatory. In 1900, he won the Anton Rubinstein Competition (in composition), the same competition that Lhévinne won in 1895 (in piano), and in which Bartók won second prize in 1905 (in piano). The performer should portray a feeling of nimbleness and lightness throughout this cheerful piece. Keep the staccatos light and crisp, while maintaining the musical inflection in the performance. Notes have been redistributed between hands in measures 8, 16, 17, 19, 32 and 40.

Fugue (Zipoli)

Zipoli was a Baroque composer from Italy, who primarily wrote keyboard music. As a Jesuit musician and missionary, he was sent to Buenos Aires in 1717 where he continued his work as a composer and church musician. The eighth notes should be played detached, while the quarter notes and sixteenth notes should be played legato. The melodic lines should be musically phrased. It is essential to slightly stress the first beat of each measures. Fingering, dynamics and tempo indications are editorial.

Sonatina No. 3 in C Major (Latour)

Jean Théodore Latour was born in France and moved to London later in his life to be the official pianist for King George IV. This work is from *Four Progressive Sonatinas* for the pianoforte, published in Baltimore in the 1820s. This sonatina features a cheerful *allegretto*, a lyrical *andante* second movement, and a rollicking *rondo* that concludes the work. Note that much of this music requires inflections of the musical line, just as the human voice inflects when one speaks. In the second movement, the short cadenzas in measures 24 and 30 should be performed expressively and freely. The *rondo* is in **A B A** form, and can be a vehicle to display the pianist's exuberance in the performance of this joyful music.

Restlessness, Op. 100, No. 18 (Burgmüller)

Born in Germany, pianist and composer Johann Friedrich Burgmüller moved to Paris later in his life, where he developed a unique style of very light piano playing. Pieces from his Op. 100 have become some of the most popular piano pieces for intermediate pianists. *Restlessness* is a study in playing rapidly and lightly, which demonstrates exactly the light style of playing for which Burgmuller was famous. Keep the left-hand chords soft, and voiced toward the top of the chord. The performer should pay special attention to the right-hand fingering.

Love Song (Bartók)

This piece clearly shows Bartók's interest in the folk music of Eastern Europe. It presents a harmonization of a Hungarian folk tune followed by a rich variation. This soulful piece provides a study in the left hand moving across the keyboard, and is No. 17 in Bartók's *For Children*, Book 1.

Trumpet Tune in C Major

Henry Purcell (1659–1695)
ZT 698

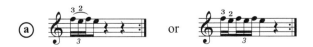

Sonatina in G Major

I.

Ludwig van Beethoven (1770–1827)
Anh. 5, No. 1

(Moderato)

(a) Appogiaturas may be played either on the beat as sixteenth notes or very quickly before the beat.

II.

Romanze
Moderato

The Avalanche

Stephen Heller (1813–1888)
Op. 45, No. 2

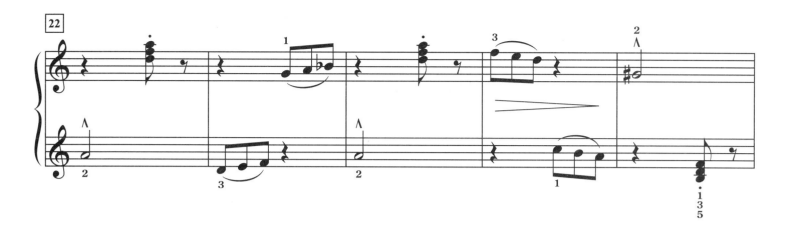

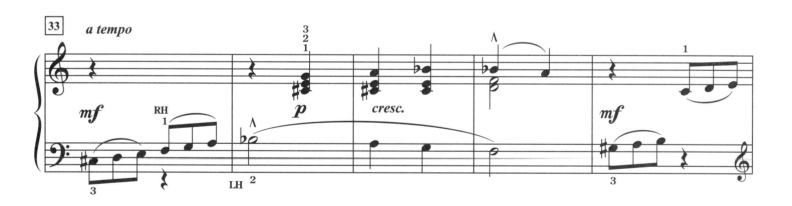

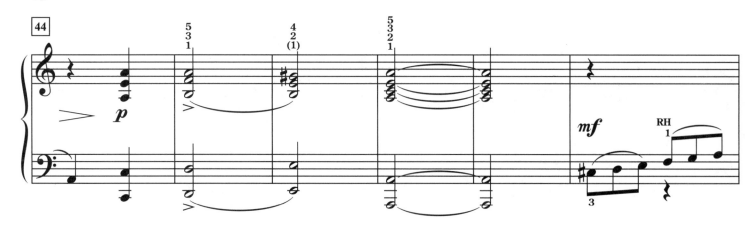

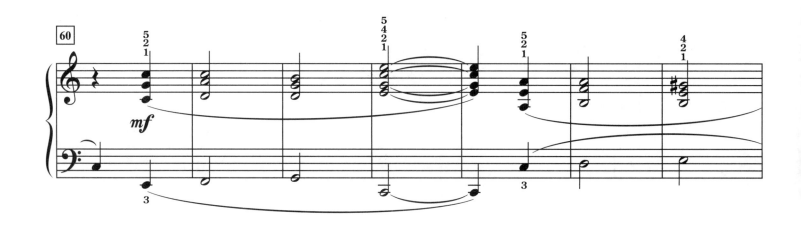

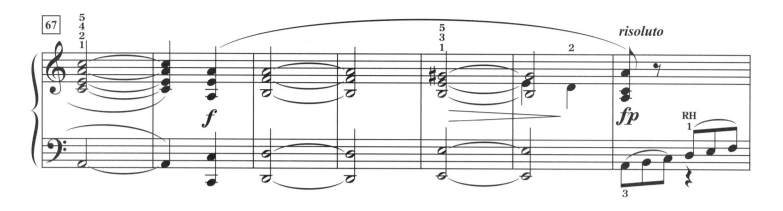

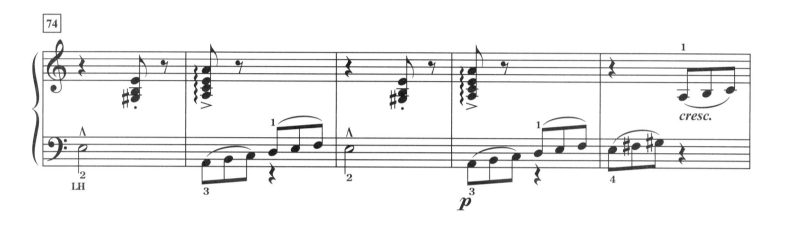

Petite Piece

Alexander Goedicke (1877–1957)
Op. 6, No. 5

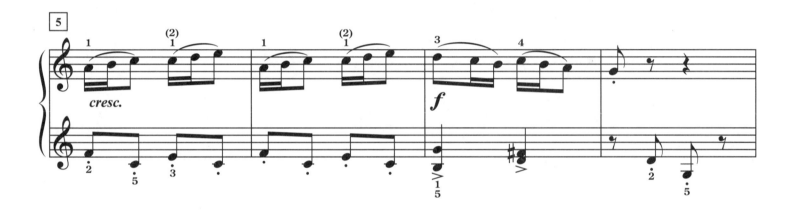

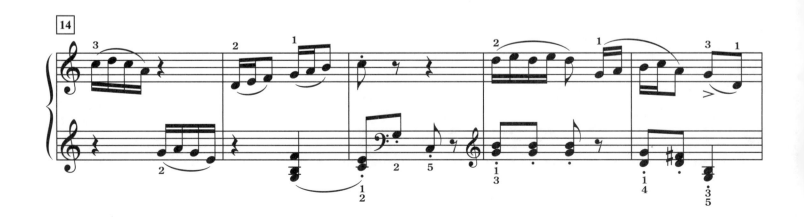

Fugue

Domenico Zipoli (1688–1726)

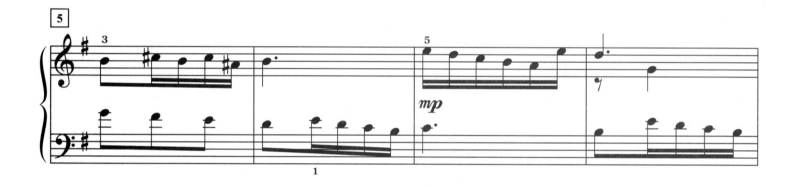

ⓐ All eighth notes should be played detached.

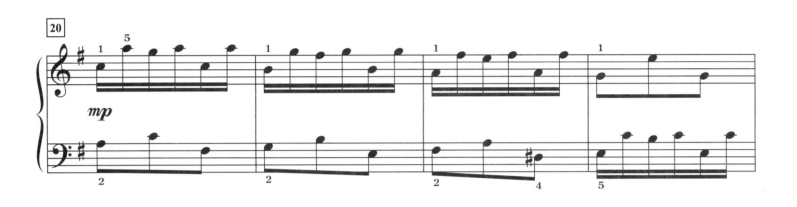

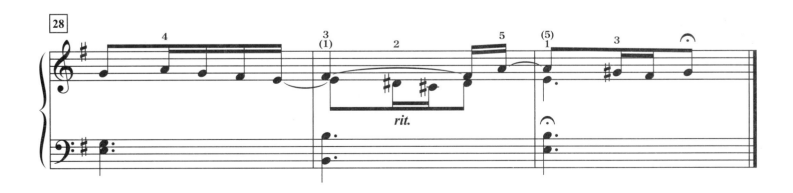

Sonatina No. 3 in C Major

I.

Jean Théodore Latour (1766–1837)

II.

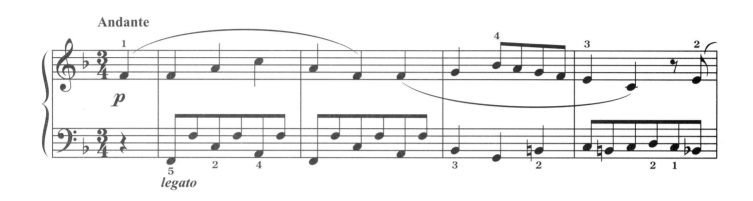

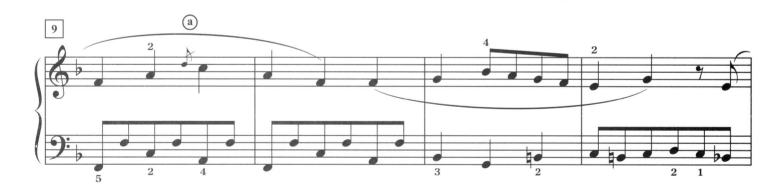

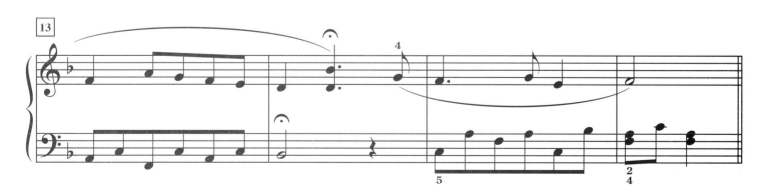

III.

Restlessness

Johann Friedrich Burgmüller (1806–1874)
Op. 100, No. 18

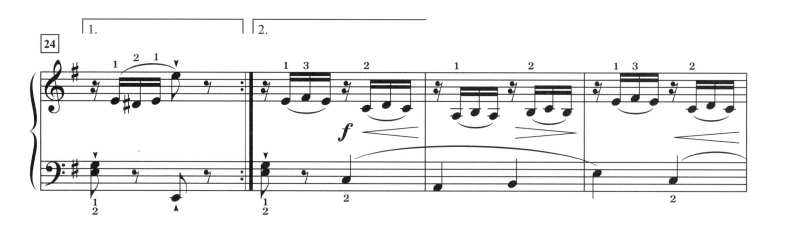

Love Song

Béla Bartók (1881–1945)